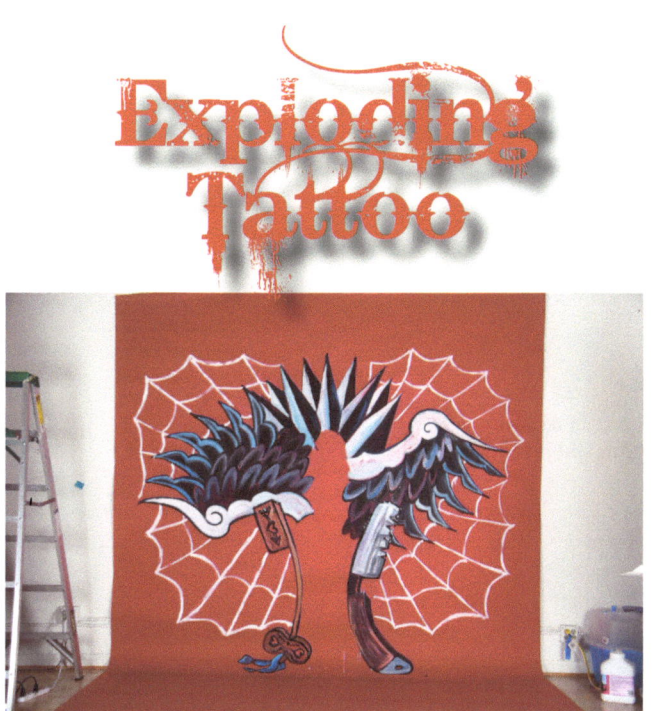

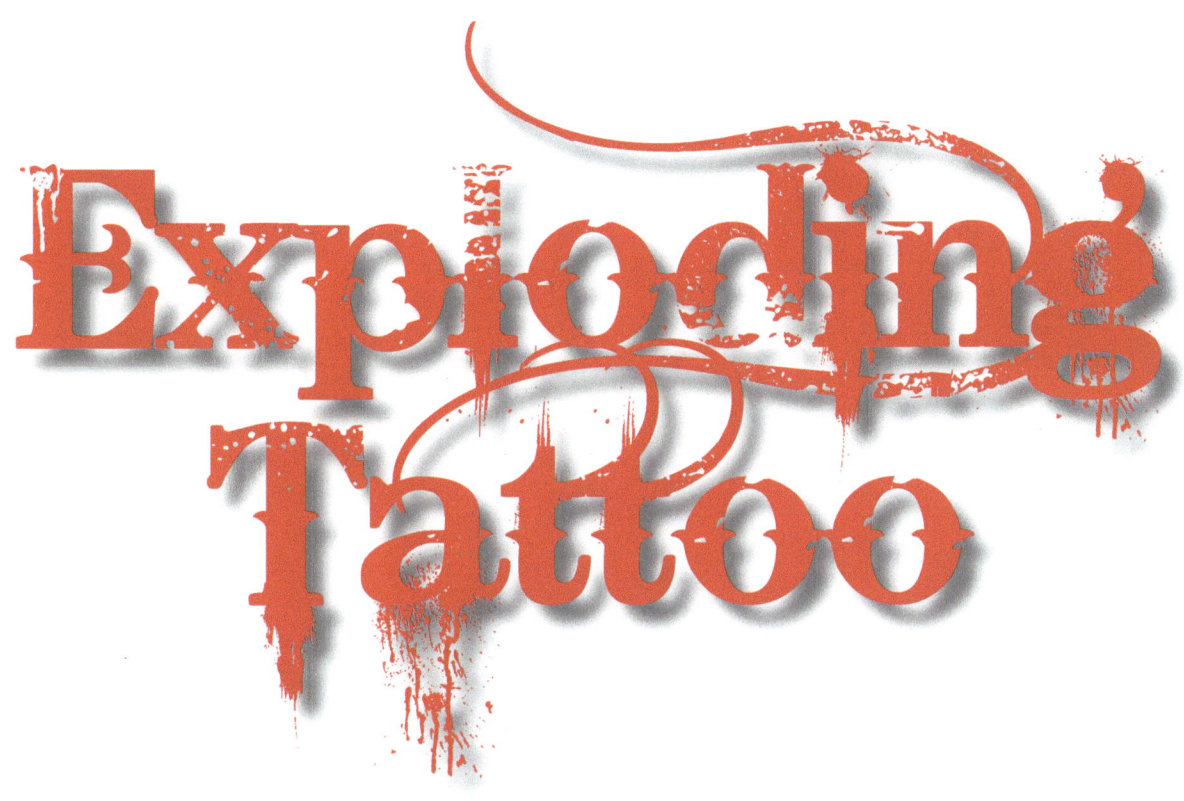

Exploding Tattoo

Ted Meyer and Anna Stump
Introduction by Dr. Teri Sowell

Tattoos in Perspective

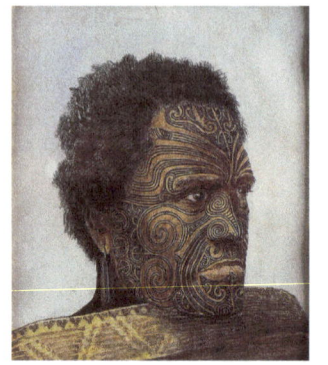

The desire to transform the human body by injecting ink under the skin is longstanding and widespread. Reasons for obtaining tattoos vary from expressing identity, status or artistic creativity, to providing protective and therapeutic powers by way of associated spiritual beliefs. The act of tattooing symbolizes a dedication to one or more of these characteristics through the endurance of physical pain and the result of a permanently altered bodyscape.

While there is evidence that ancient Europeans practiced tattooing, it remained dormant until the end of the 18th century when Western sailors began returning home from distant Polynesian islands sporting tattoo souvenirs. It created a fashion stir among the European elite and introduced a new word into the English language, tattoo, which originates from the Tahitian word tatau. Now firmly entrenched in our contemporary Western world, tattoo has proven to be an elastic form of artistic self-expression.

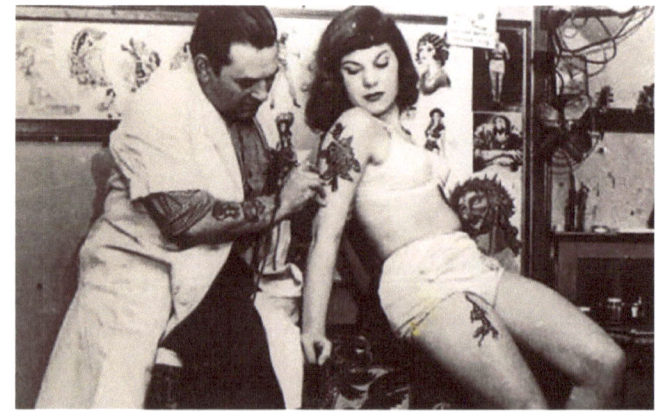

Since the skin mediates between our inner self and our projected social persona, technologies such as tattoo allow people to artistically compose and perform their social selves. By using the skin to proclaim love, faith, devotion, power, fear, strength, beauty, heritage, history and/or fashion, people are able not only to construct, but also control their identity, while situating themselves into a wider social world. When revealed, tattoos create a social disruption. The visual noise created by inked skin is part of the overall performance, but like all performance art, meanings will change depending on audience and context.

Ted Meyer and Anna Stump's Exploding Tattoos creates an elaborate restaging of the symbolic self. Drawing upon the emotional and visual power of the original inked composition, Meyer and Stump are able to transform the everyday performance of tattoo revelation and reception into a spectacle by embellishing the context and widening the audience through photographic reproduction. Like all good spectacles, the tattoos exploding on the following pages demand attention as remarkable visual performances.

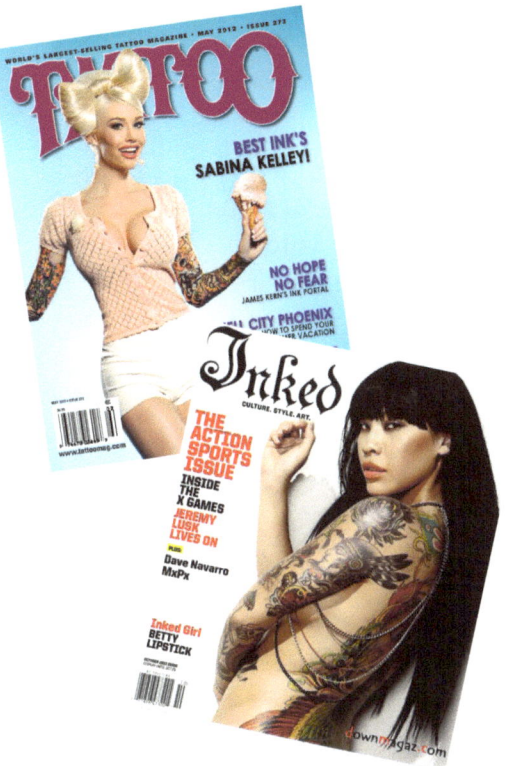

Dr. Teri Sowell

Dr. Teri Sowell teaches African, Pacific Island and Native American Art History, as well as Ritual Theory and Curatorial Studies, at the University of California San Diego. She specializes in Polynesian tattoos, past and present, from New Zealand to Los Angeles, and has managed to collect quite a few along the way.

The Process

In 2010 we were sitting around our studio in Downtown Los Angeles, talking about how to reach a broader audience with our painting. Who collects art

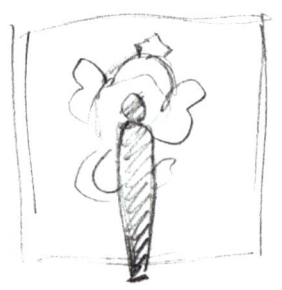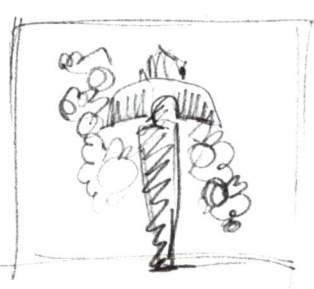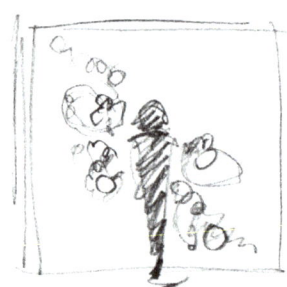

these days? We are both interested in figuration, and it dawned on us that many Southern Californians are buying art for their bodies rather than for their living spaces. Could we capture

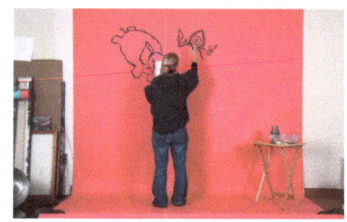

the art of tattooing with painting and photography that somehow engulfed the subject? Our continuing series, "Exploding Tattoo," was born.

Our process starts with models; friends, strangers we meet in the grocery, Facebook acquaintances, or art fans who lift up their shirts to reveal colorful artwork. We prefer large, unique or thematically

linked tattoos. The model comes to the studio and we adjust our design to the meanings of and stories behind the tattoos. We work with acrylic paint on nine-foot wide photo-backdrop paper. The process is photographed at different intervals to find the model's best pose (which also helps him or her relax and become part of the art-making). The entire project takes three to four hours to complete, culminating in the best photograph as the final product.

We also create "Exploding Tattoos" as a live

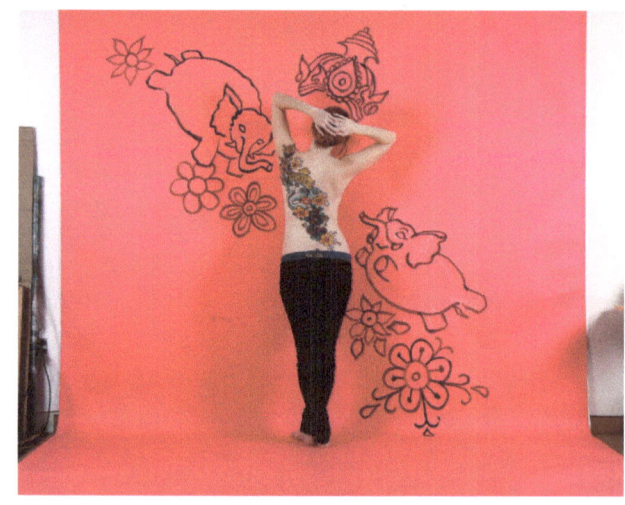

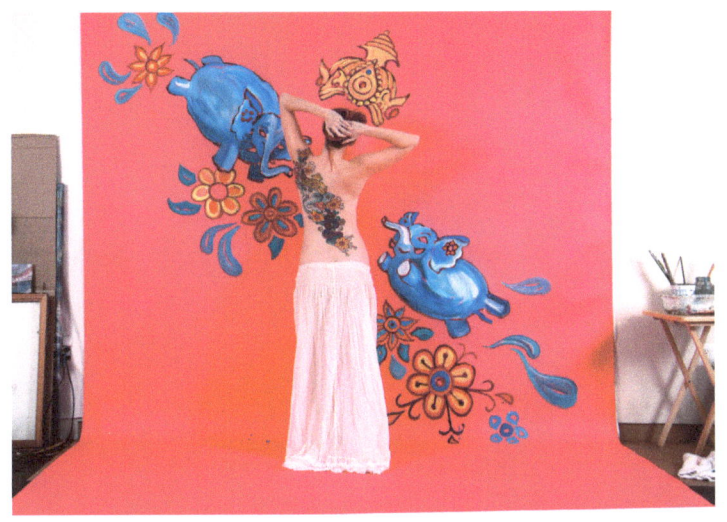

performance at galleries, art fairs, and other public events. The process is the same, although hundreds of people may be watching over the hours as the painting and photography progresses. Audience members love to pose for their own snatshots in front of the completed painting.

As the series has progressed, themes have emerged. We are exploring the Southern California fixation on the body, which includes decoration with ink and piercing, manipulation through surgery, diet and exercise, and even tanning, dyeing, and shaving. We are fascinated by how tattoo decoration appropriates pop imagery from other cultures and religions. Many of our models

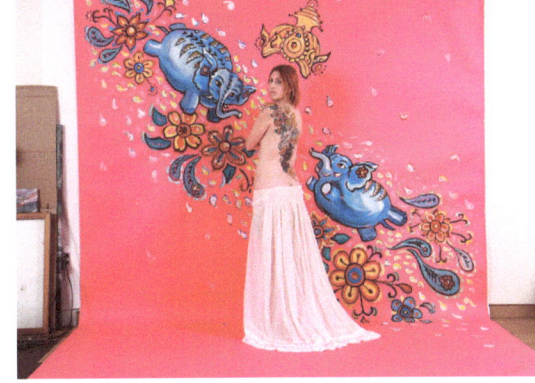

have spiritual connects to their tattoo designs, or intimate stories that inspired the imagery. Some of our models designed their own tattoos, others "collect" a specific tattoo artist. Some tattoo designs are copied repeatedly, reminding us of medieval manuscript copybooks, where variations resulted in regional styles.

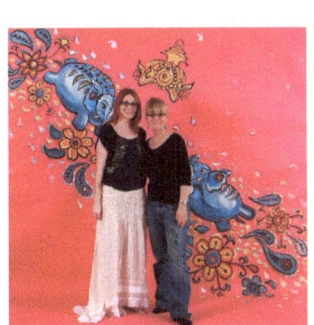

In "Exploding Tattoo" the body interacts with patterns of itself, an image of an image. We celebrate these New Collectors, allowing our models to be surrounded by the world they carry on their skin.

We would like to thank all the models who have posed for our project, and invite commissions for new "Exploding Tattoos".

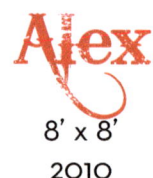

Alex

8' x 8'

2010

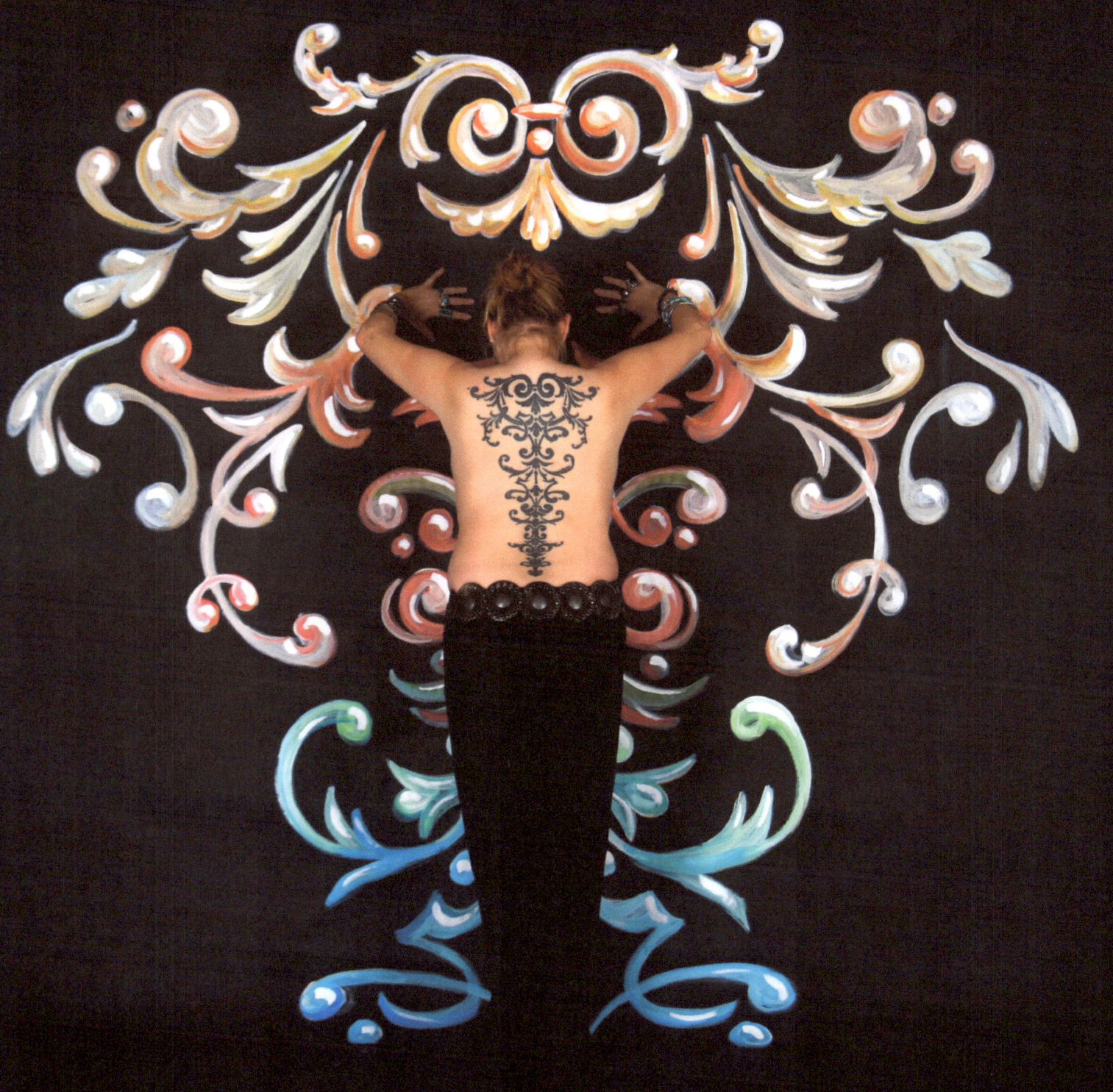

8' x 8'

2012

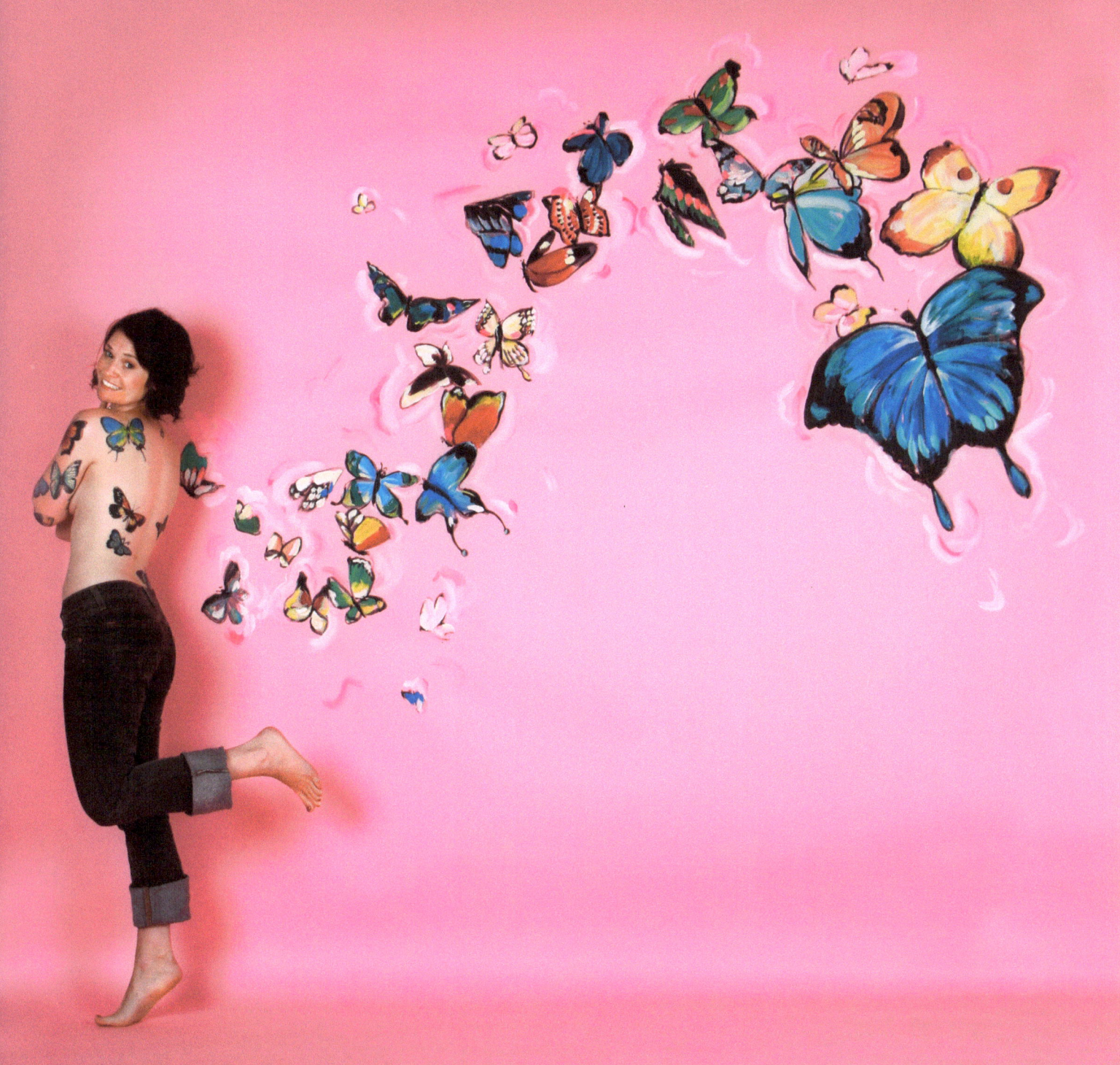

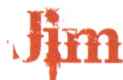

Jim

8' x 8'

2010

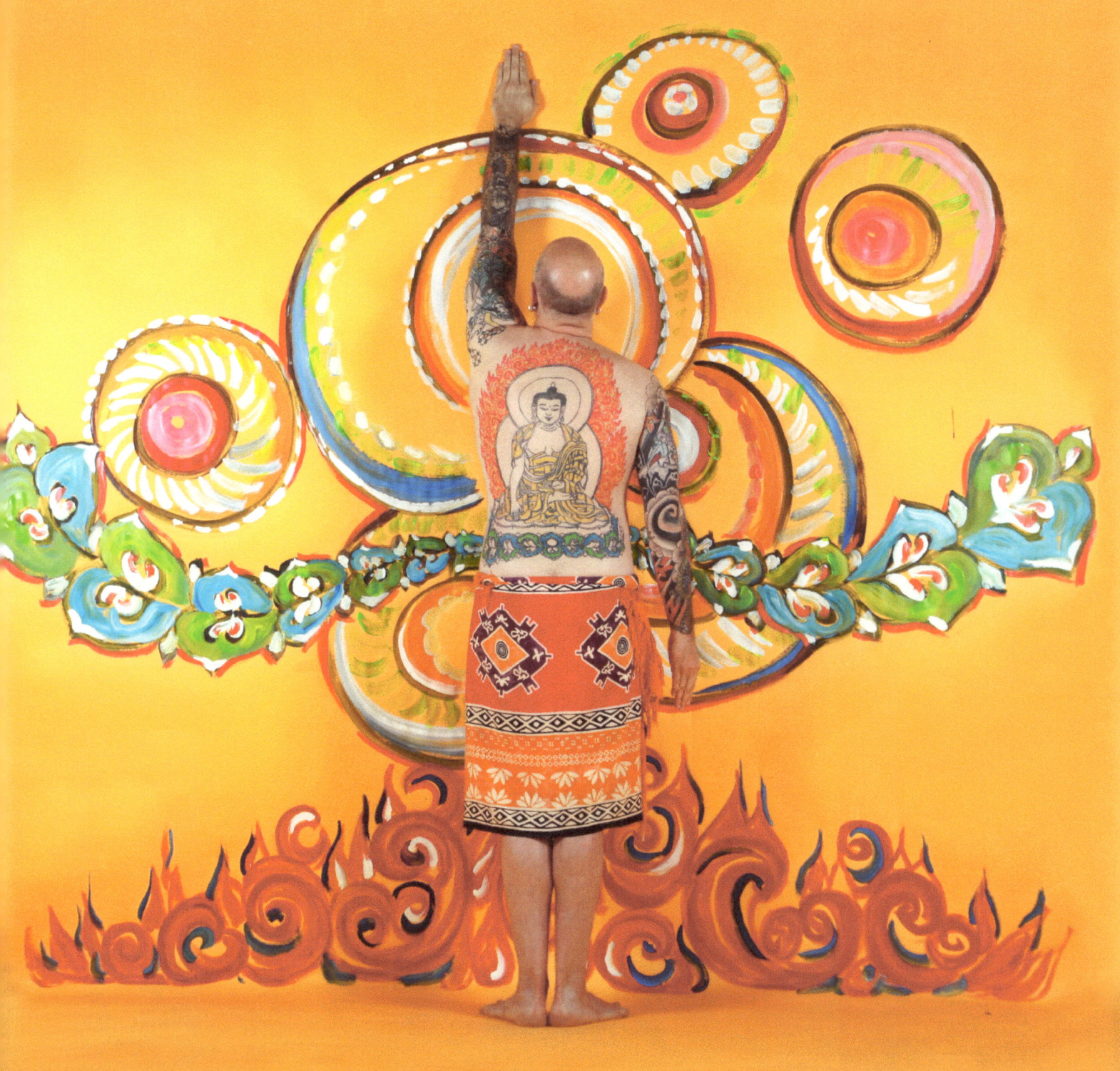

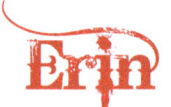

8' x 8'

2010

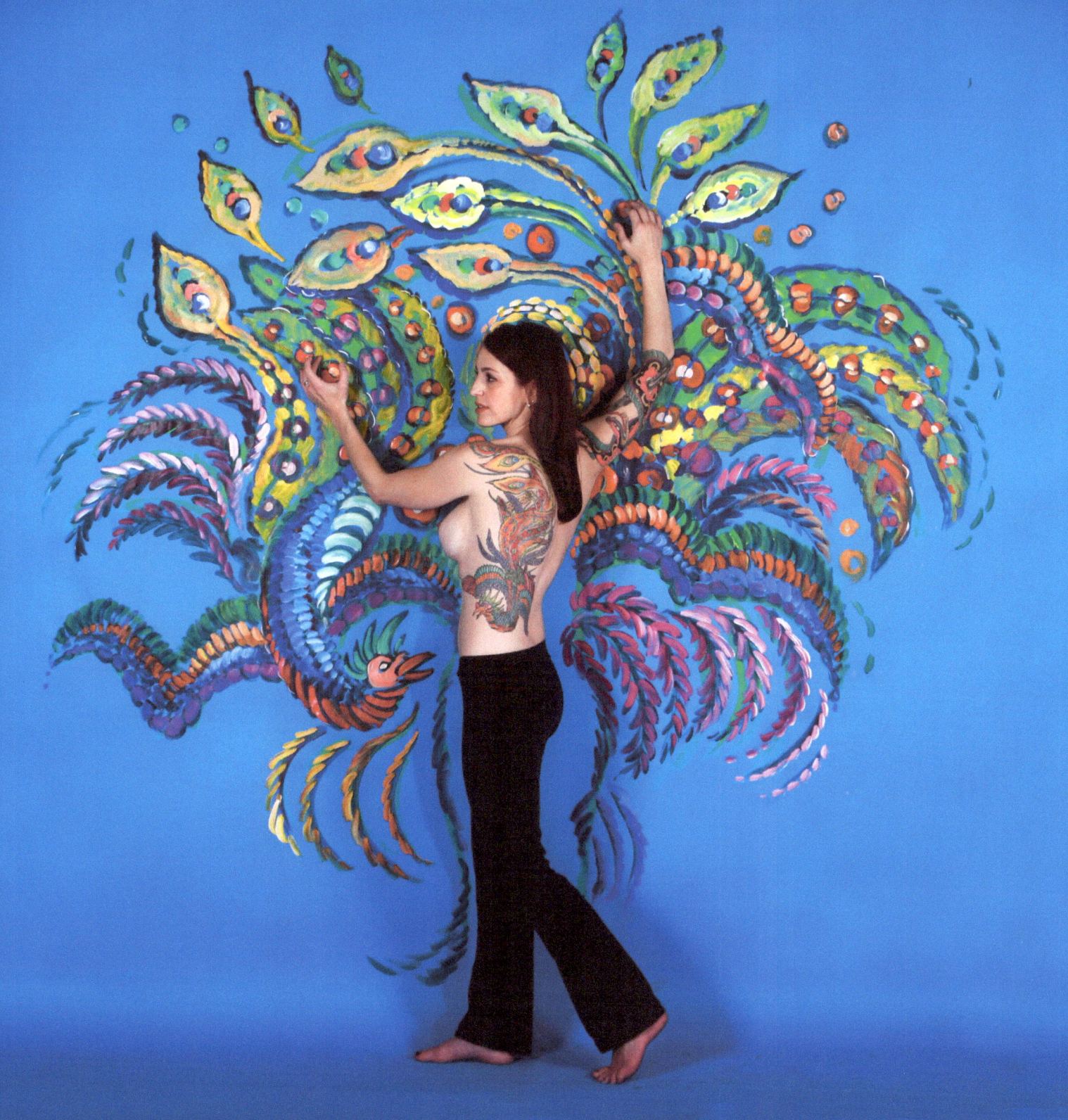

Turtle

8' x 8'

2011

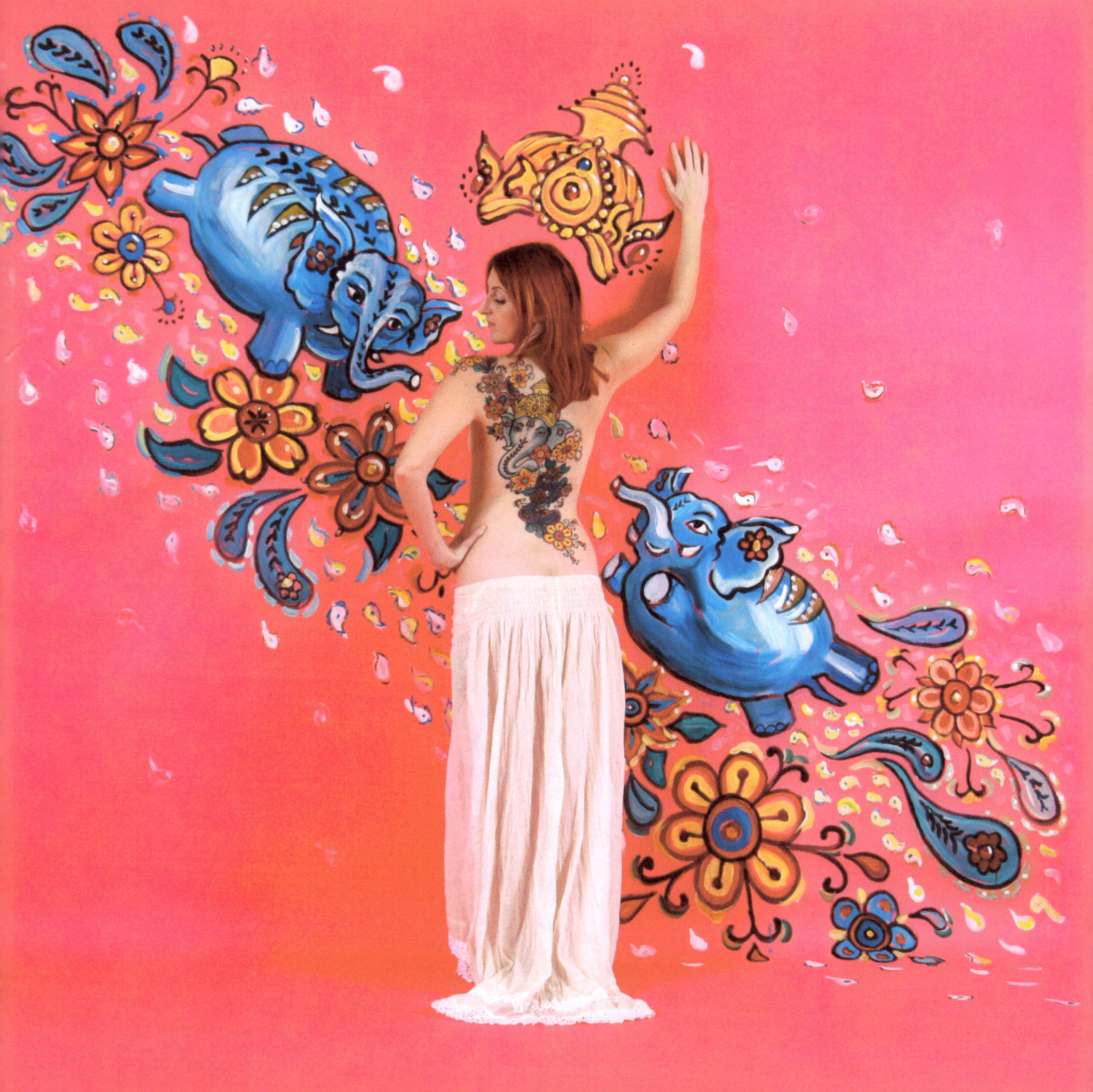

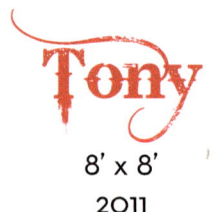

Tony

8' x 8'

2011

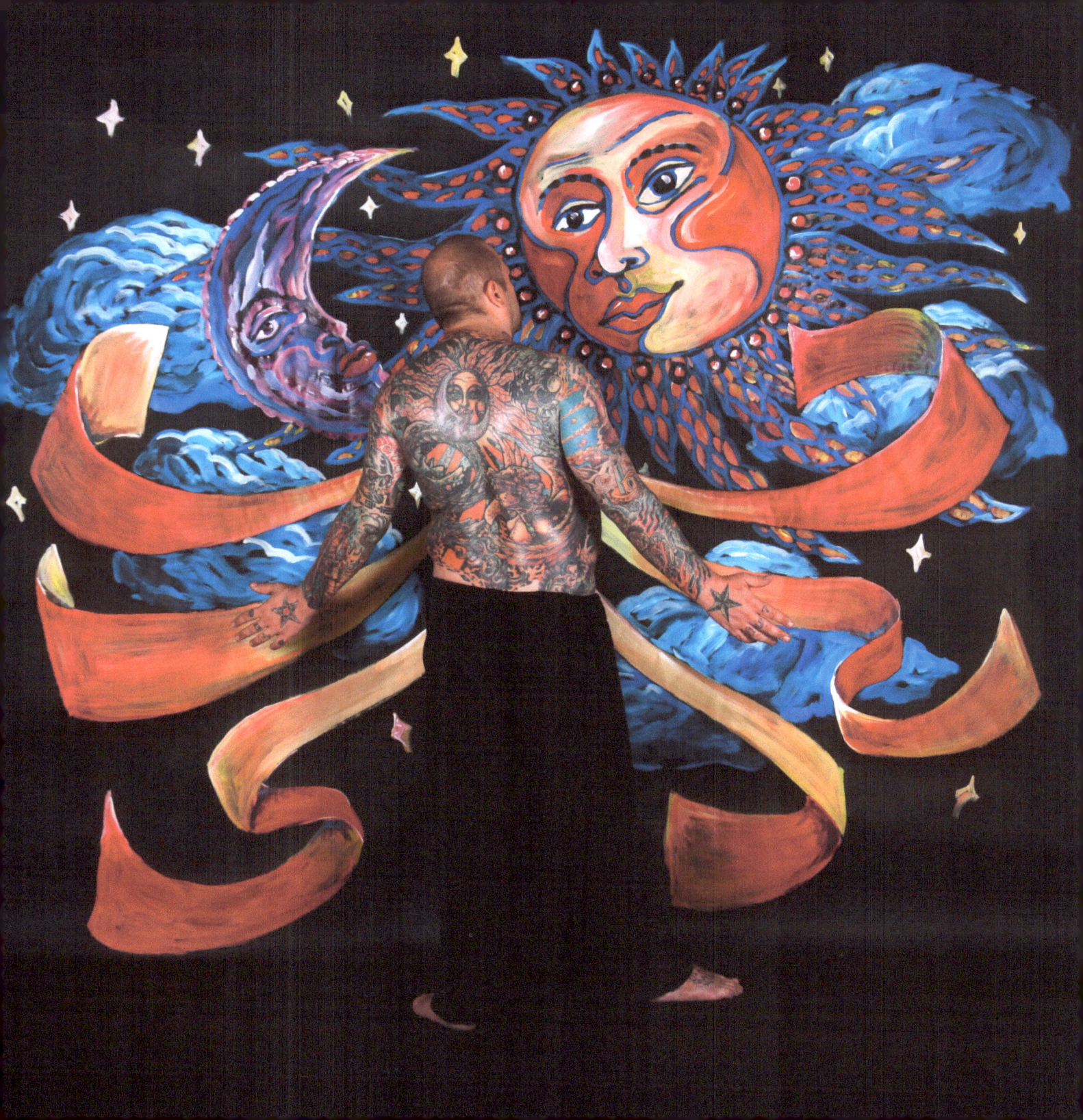

Anne

8' x 8'

2012

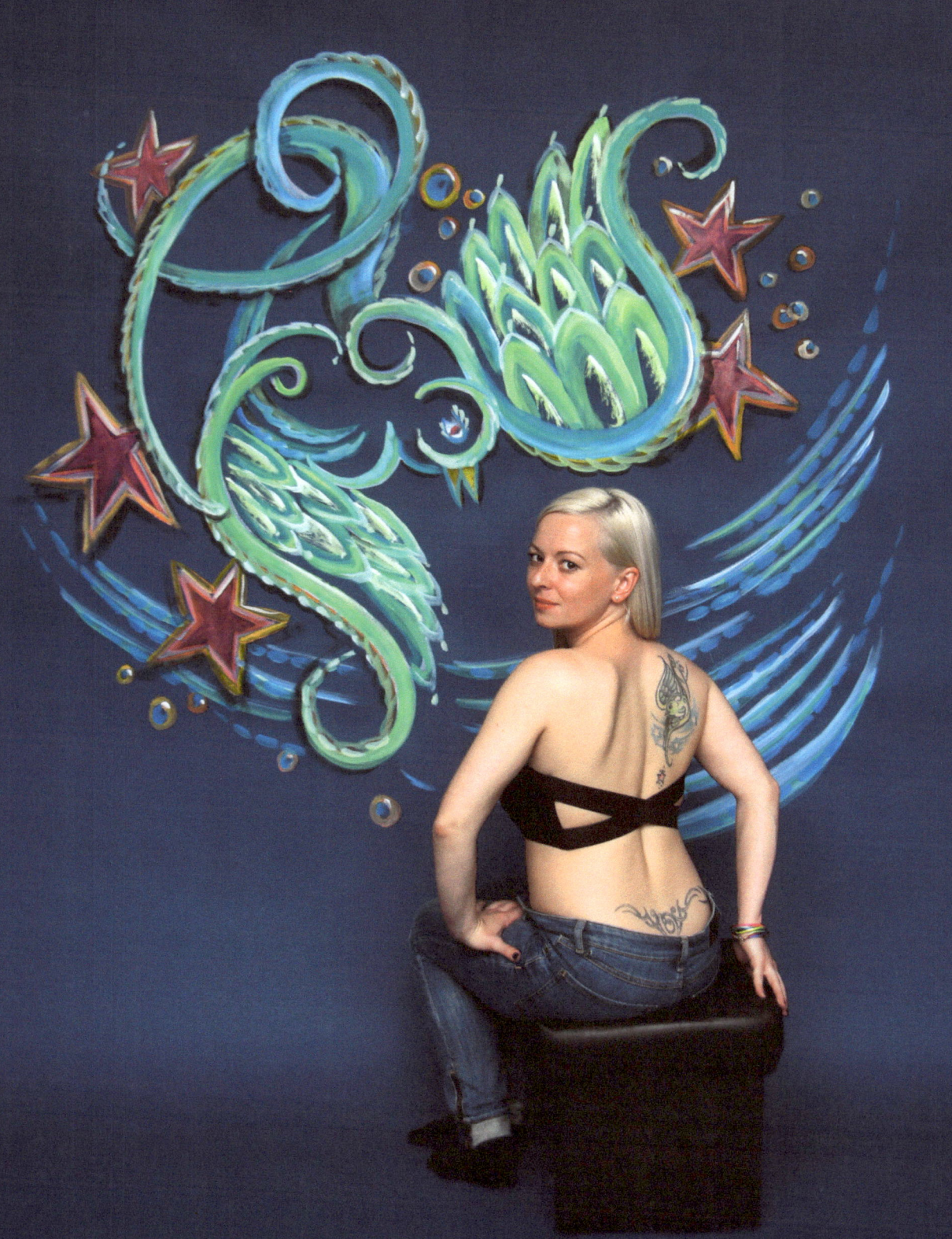

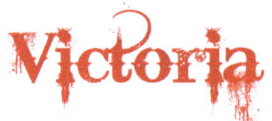

8' x 8'

2013

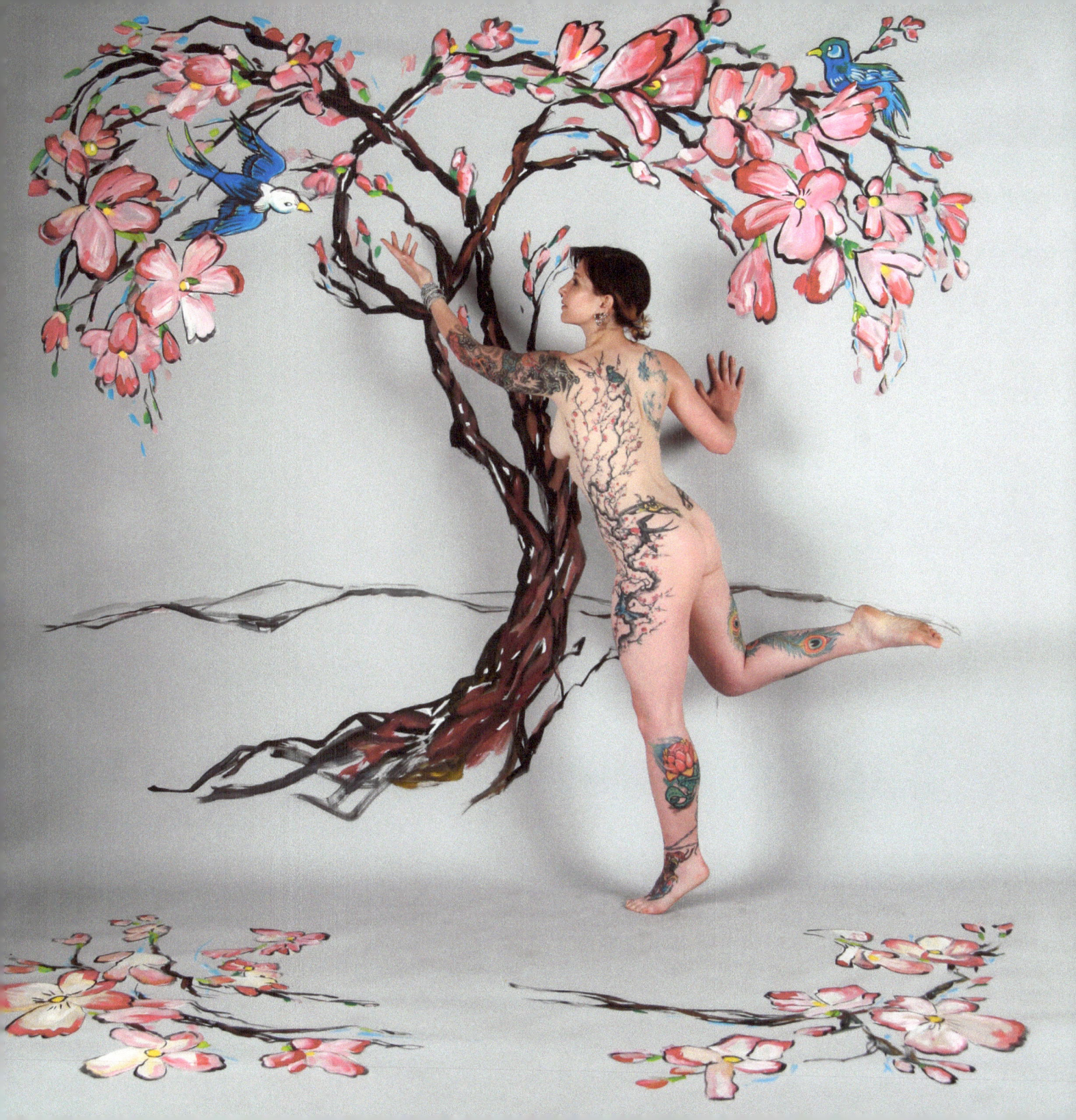

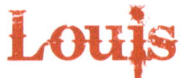

8' x 8'

2011

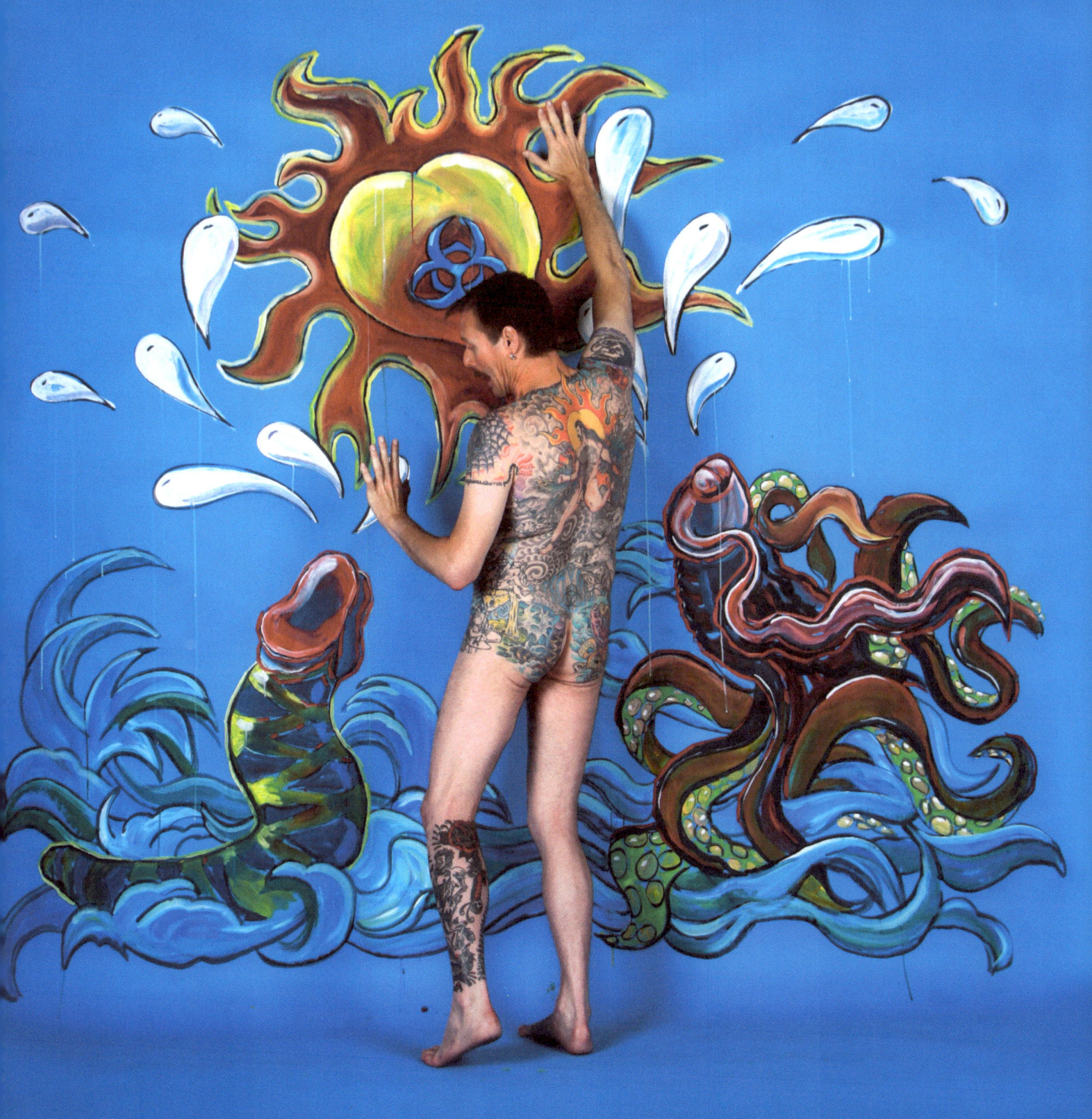

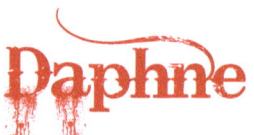

8' x 8'

2010

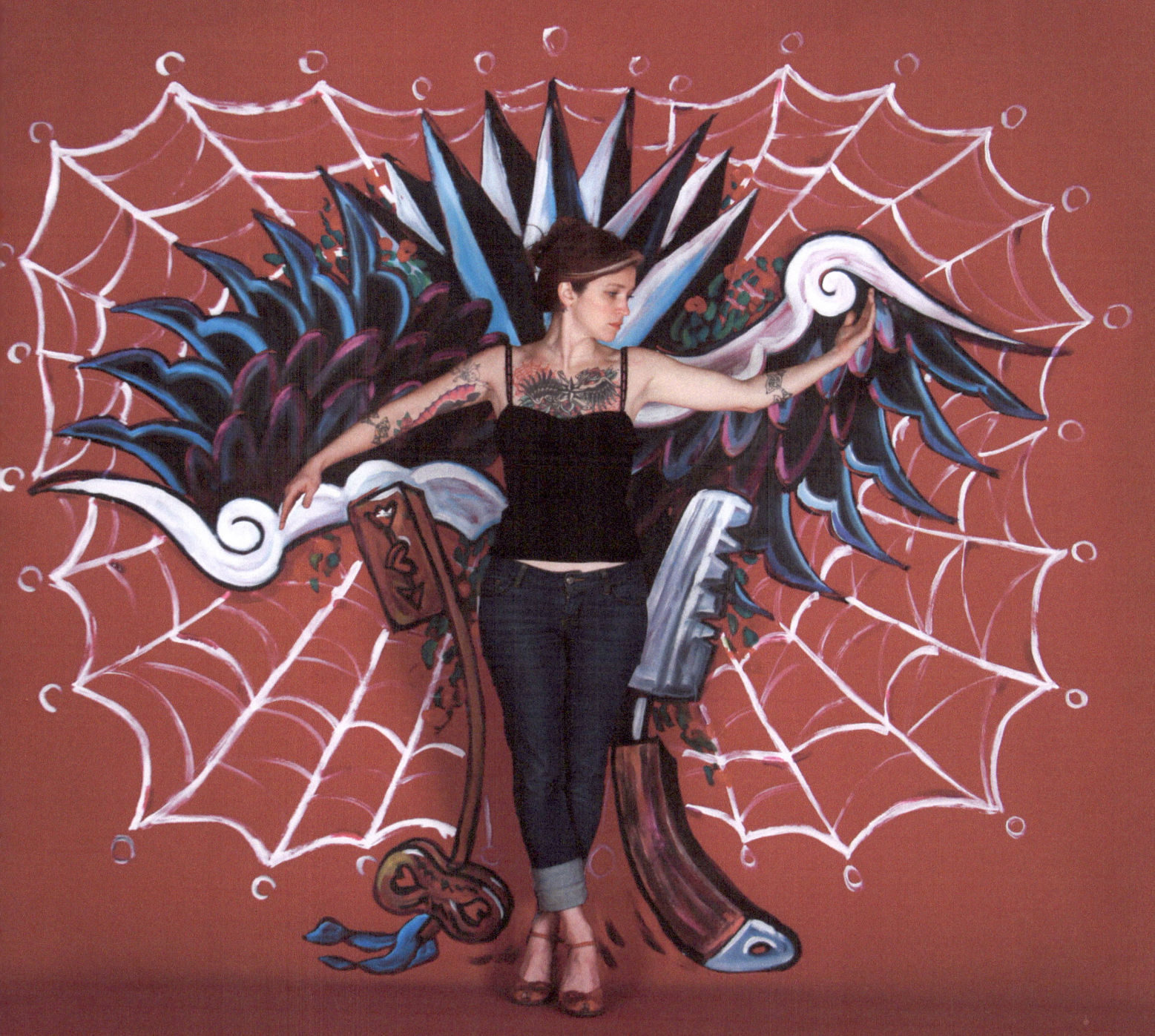

Mitzi & Michael

8' x 8'

2013

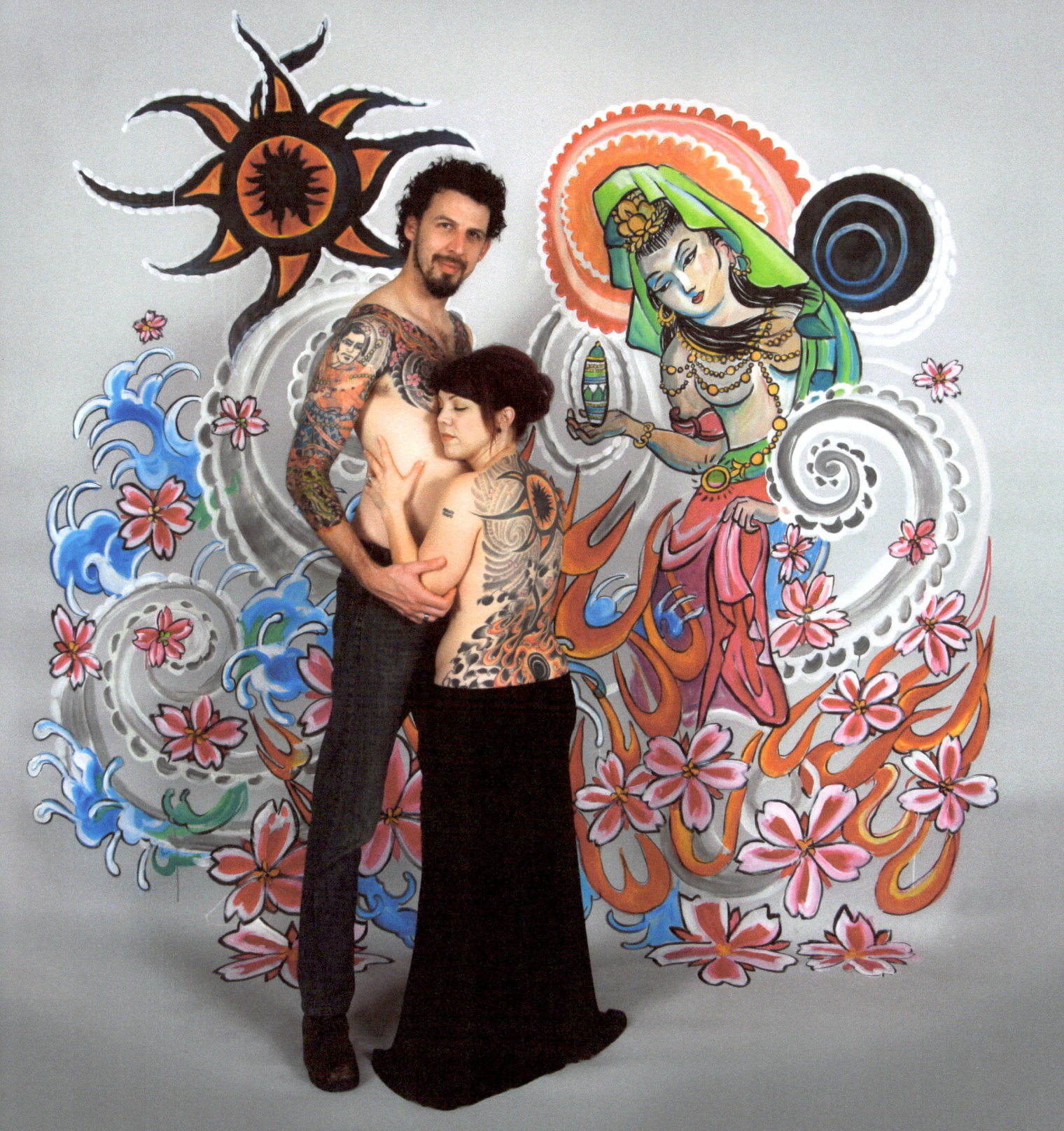

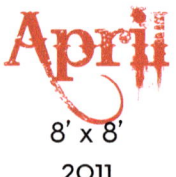

April

8' x 8'

2011

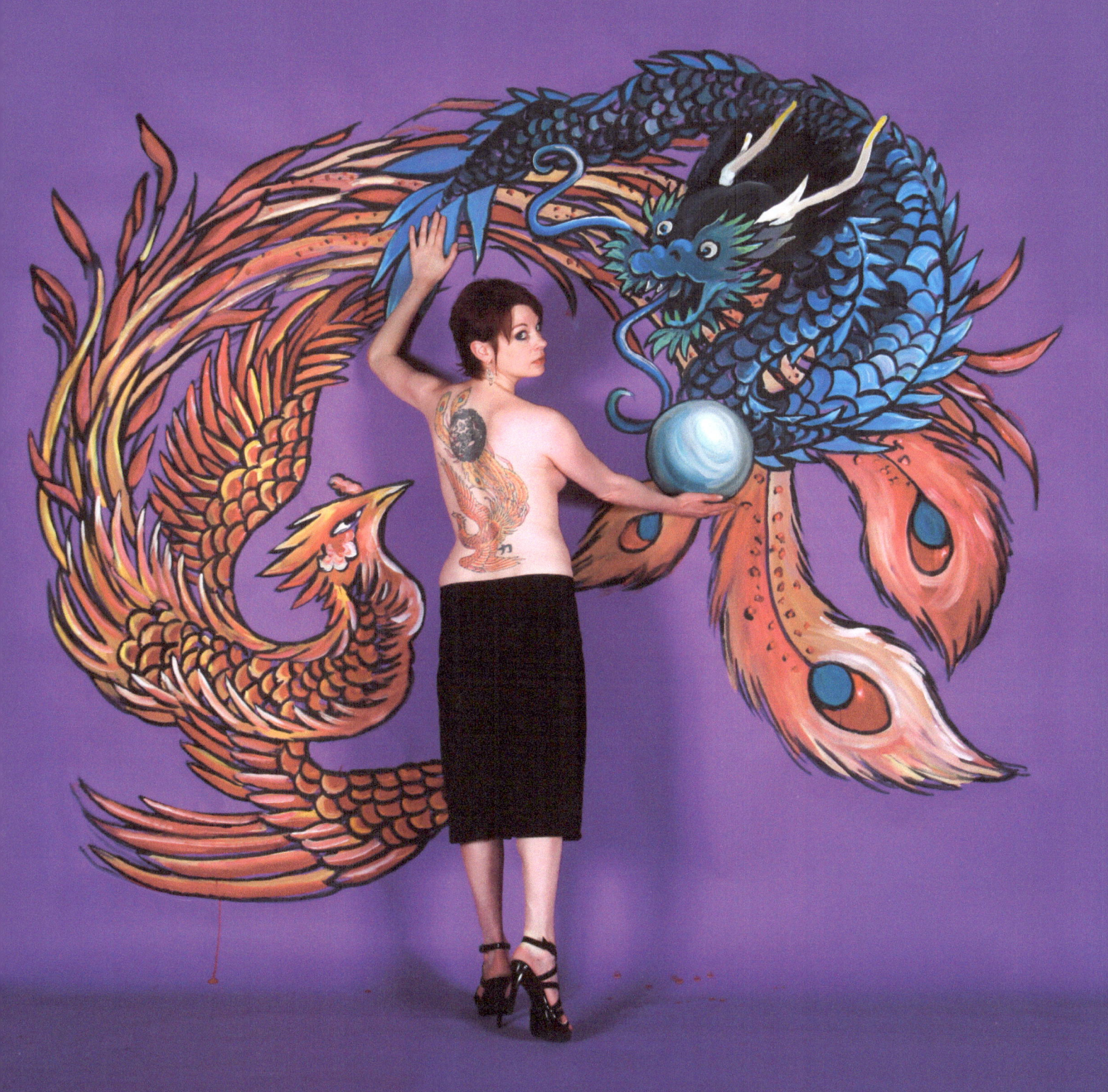

Katie & Gerardo

8' x 8'

2011

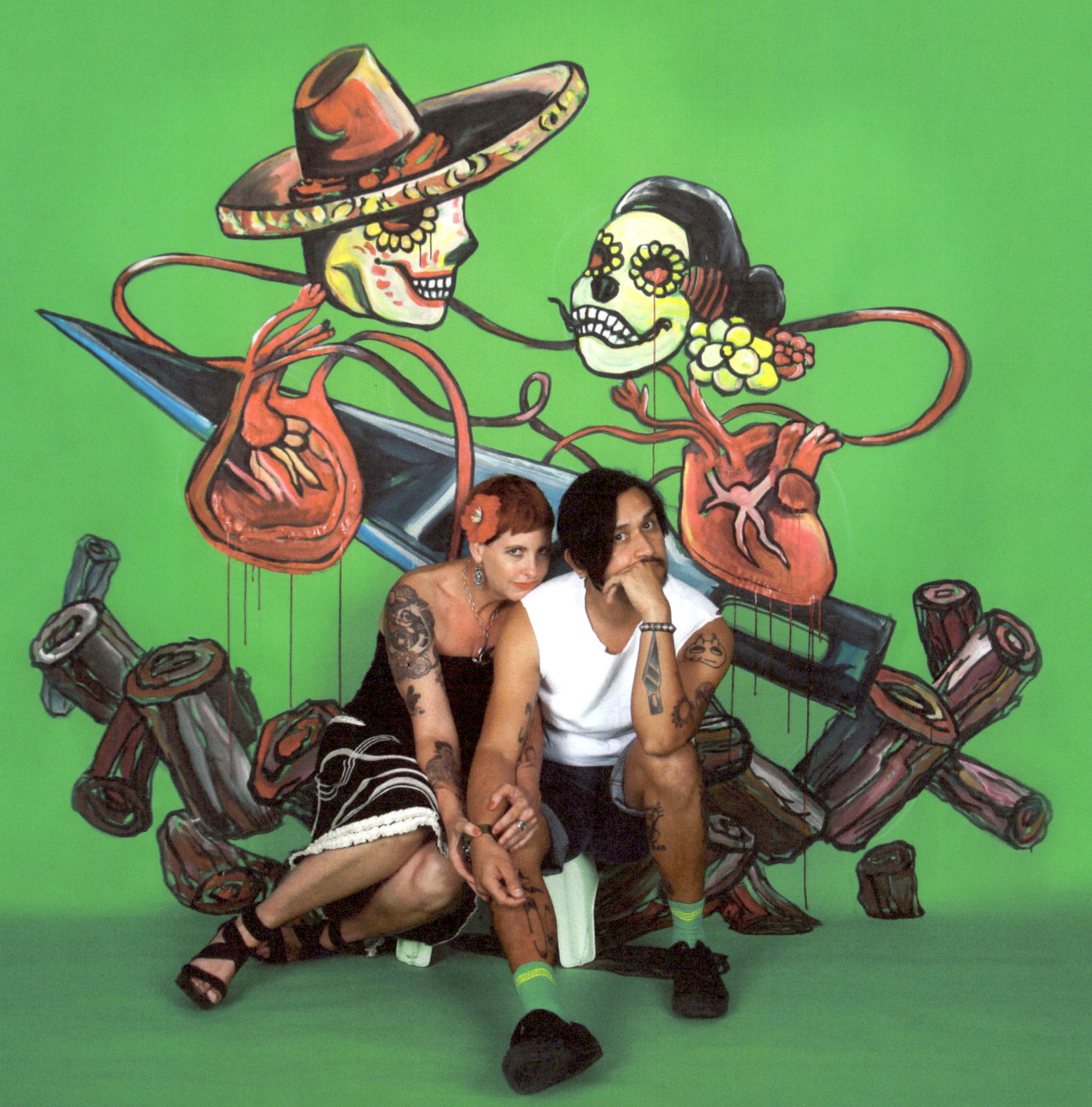

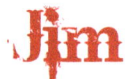

9' x 9'

2012

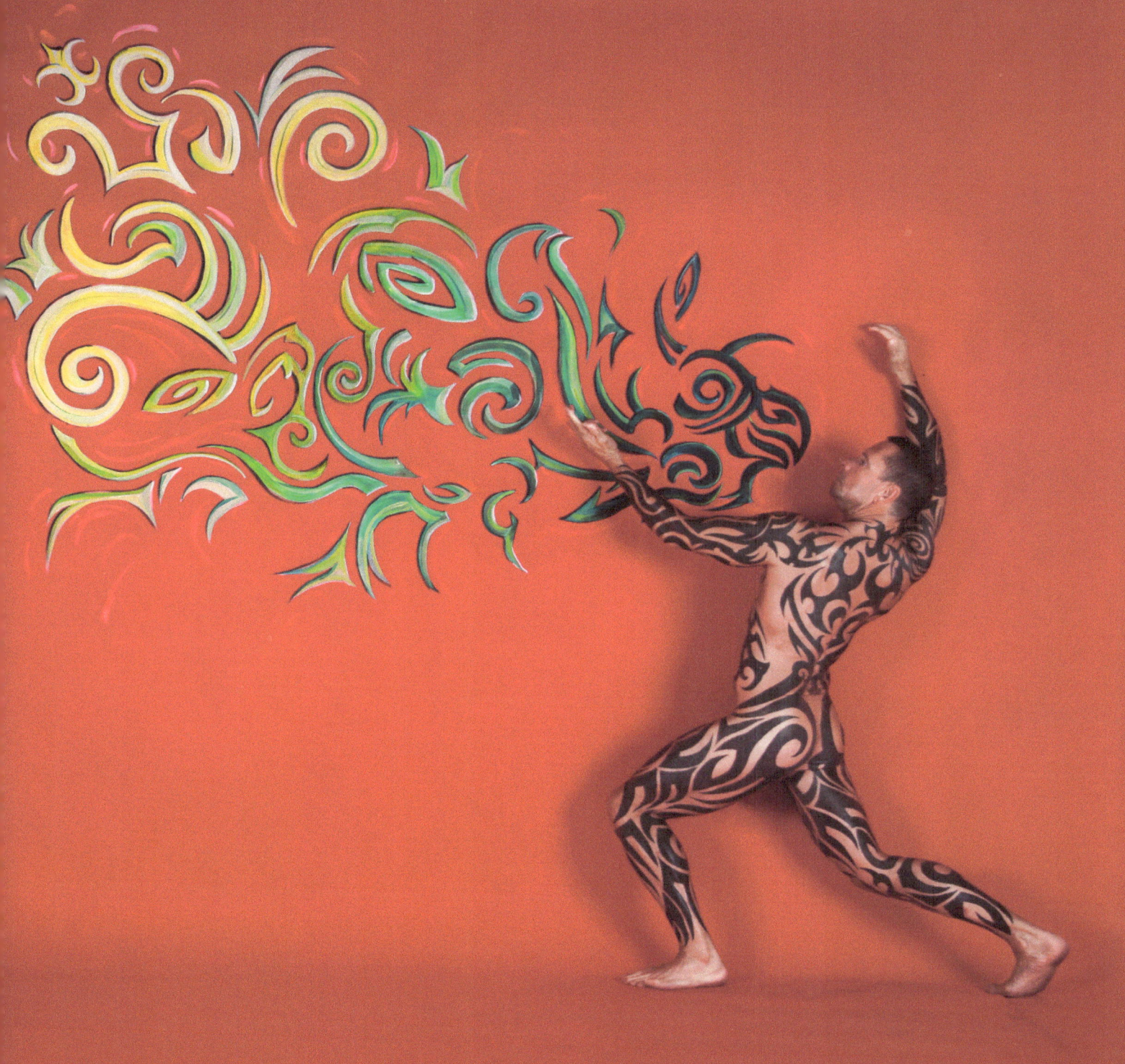

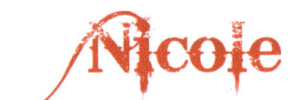

8' x 8'

2012

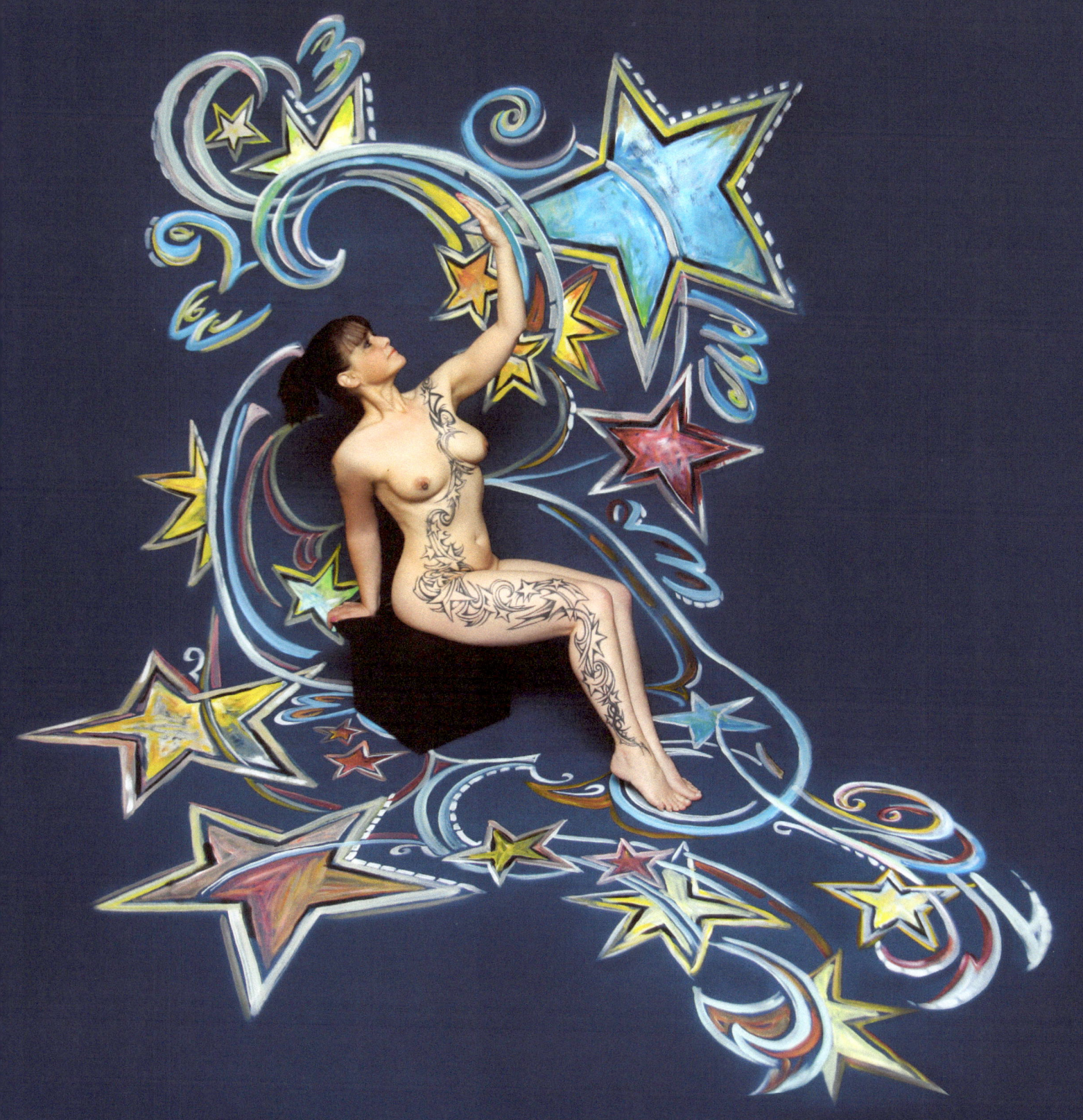

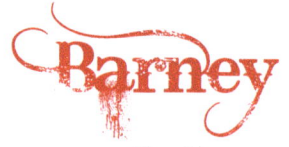

8' x 8'

2011

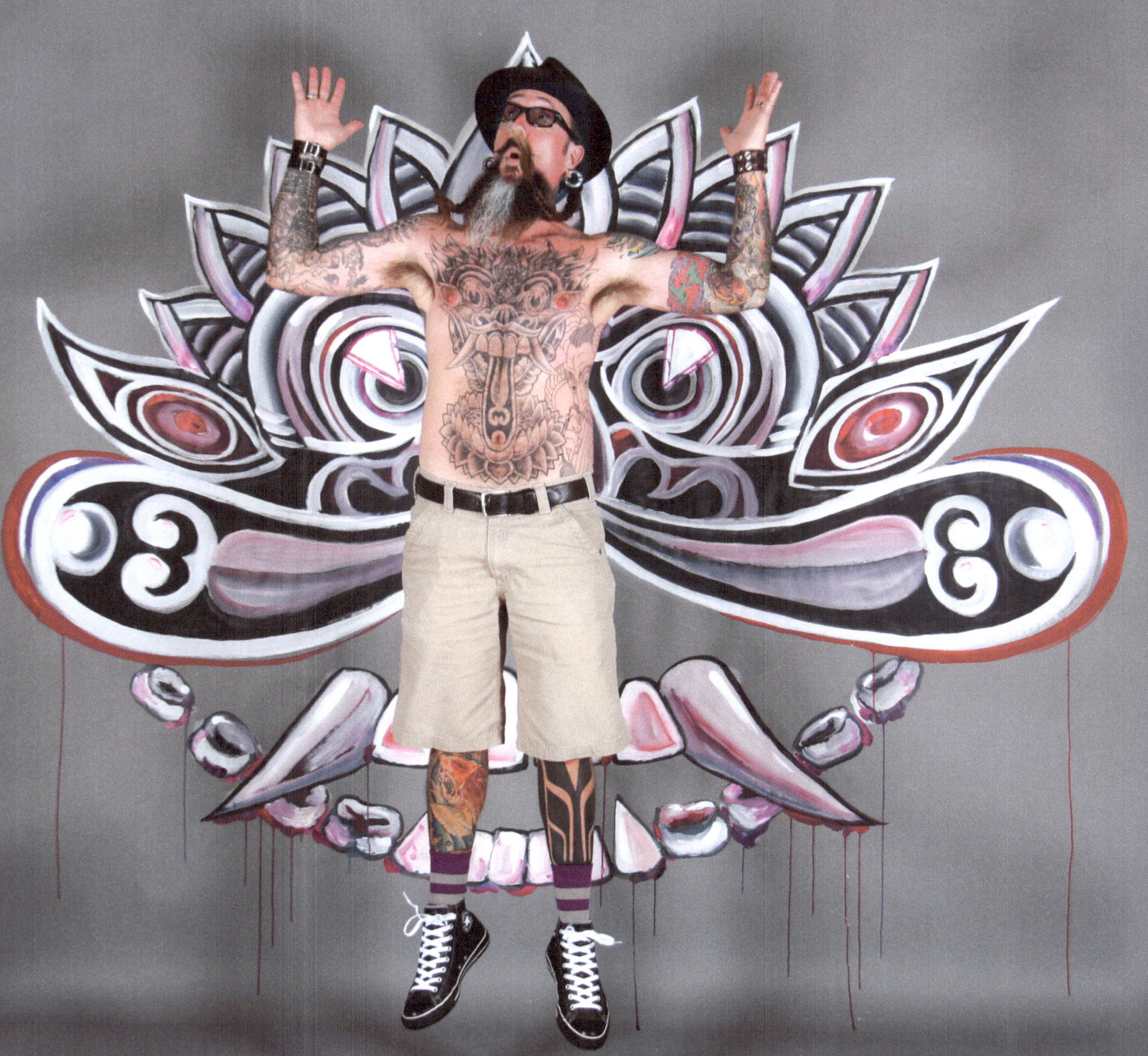

8' x 8'

2012

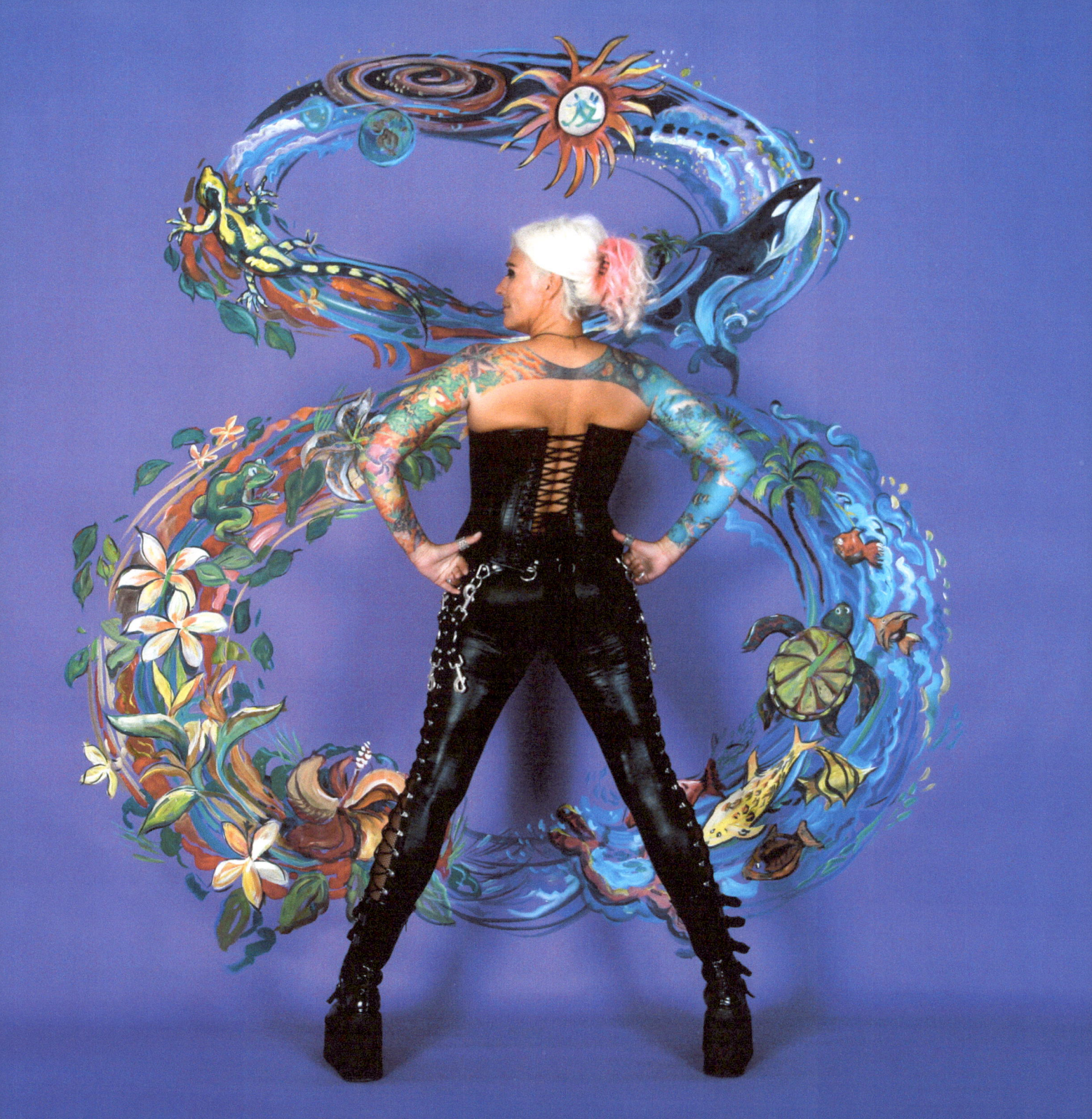

Ted Meyer

Ted Meyer won his first art show at age 6 after copying a flamingo that one of the older kids drew. The guilt of this image appropriation has followed him ever since.

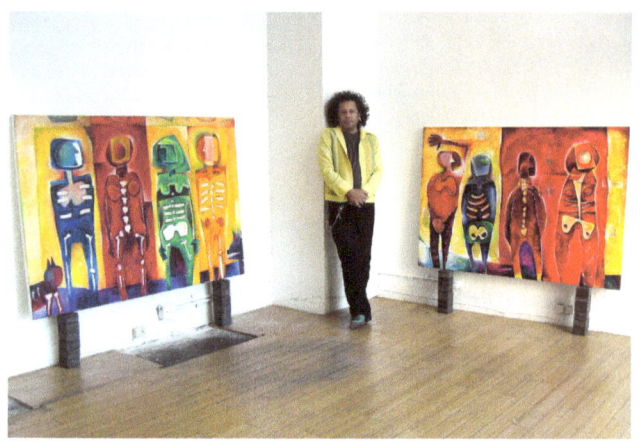

Ted started painting 1987 when a friend gave him some paint for Christmas with a card that read, "You keep saying you are an artist, paint!" Seven months later Ted sold 8 of the 11 paintings exhibited in his first show. Since that first show Ted's work has been displayed in museums on 3 continents.

Much of Ted's paintings have been influenced by his dealings with the health care system and his own health problems. Born with Gaucher's disease, often his earlier works depict contorted, pained and highly designed skeletal images. This series titled "Structural Abnormalities" was initially created in the months before his first round of hip replacements.

In recent years with his work has shifted from "Ted-centric" to images that highlight other people's health problems. His "Scarred for Life, Mono prints of Human Scars" series chronicles those events that suddenly changed people's lives.

Ted added photography to his skill set about 7 years go after a double hip replacement operation. Finding it too painful to stand and paint he started creating images in photos that mirrored his paintings, focusing on contours in multi-figure compositions. His current photo series "Girls on a Black Chair" again goes back to his painting and requires all his subject to express themselves within the confines of a single shape, this time a tall high backed black chair.

Ted is also a freelance designer, writer, photographer and illustrator. He has written and illustrated 6 books. "Shrink Yourself: The Complete do-it-Yourself Book of Freudian Psychoanalysis", "The Butt Hello - And Other Reasons My Cats Drive Me Crazy", "Cats Around the World", "Good Things You Can Learn from A Bad Relationship" " Scarred for Life" and "50 States of Cats". He is the owner of Art Your World, a full service design studio.

Ted is a Visting Scholar at the National Museum of Health and Medicine in Washington, DC. He is currently the Artist-in-Residence at the UCLA Geffen School of Medicine. He has held teaching positions at Brooks College in Long Beach, CA and California State University at Northridge. Ted also speaks to patient and Doctor groups on the effects of health on art.

www.TedMeyer.com

Anna Stump

Anna Stump is an artist and arts educator living in San Diego. She earned her Bachelor's degree at Occidental College and her Master of Fine Arts at San Diego State University. She was a Senior Fulbright Scholar to the Fine Arts Department at Anadolu University in Eskisehir, Turkey in 2006-2007. She teaches studio and art history courses at San Diego City College and Grossmont College.

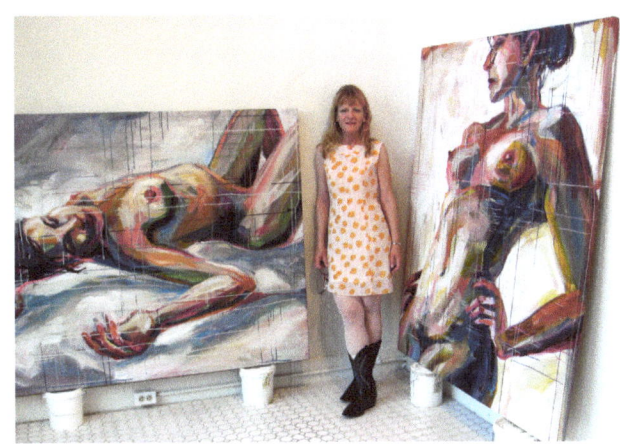

Anna's New York Times reviewed blog of three years, Kloe Among the Turks, examines the art scene in Southern California and Turkey, as well as issues of arts education. In 2009 she curated an exhibition of 130 artists from Southern California and Turkey, presented in San Diego, Los Angeles, Istanbul and Ankara.

Anna is the founder of the San Diego Feminist Image Group. She is a member of Mid-Air Trio, an improvisational group that combines painting, dance and soundscapes in live performances. She is one-half of the painting team Hill&Stump. The artist is represented by MLA Gallery in Los Angeles, Sanatyapim Gallery in Ankara, Turkey, and Sparks Gallery in San Diego. She was recently profiled in the Huffington Post by Mat Gleason for her new work, "Sexy Jesus."

"My work as a painter, performance artist, and curator is intimately connected. Interest in body politics, feminism, and physicality is grounded in community building and education, which I challenge personally by cultural risk-taking. My job is to both please and provoke."

AnnaStump.com
HillandStump.com

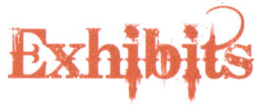 Exhibits

Boyd, Los Angeles
exhibition
2011

Loft at Liz's, Los Angeles
performance and exhibition
2011

San Diego Fine Art Fair
performance
2011

Barbara's at the Brewery, Los Angeles
exhibition
2011

Philipp Scheidemann Haus , Kassel, Germany
performance
2012

Oceanside Museum of Art
performance
2012

KGB Gallery, Los Angeles
performance and exhibition
2014

www.ingramcontent.com/pod-product-compliance
Lightning Source LLC
Chambersburg PA
CBHW051102180526
45172CB00002B/744